For Eleanor Nichols—

A great editor and
a wonderful friend

Contents

Preface

Sometimes it seems as though almost every animal that can be seen with the naked eye has a superstition connected with it. And if the microscope had been invented back when these superstitions were dreamed up, there would probably be crazy beliefs about the amoeba and the paramecium.

Many of the strange ideas about animals come from the world of witchcraft. Every witch was supposed to have an animal. These weird pets, called *familiars,* came in many varieties—cats, dogs, rabbits, toads, birds, fish, or perhaps even insects. The job of the familiar was to help the witch with her little chores, such as

THE RUBBERADO bounces when shot. Anyone who eats it bounces, too
THE RACKABORE, an offspring of the javelina, is legged for sidehills. There are two types, right and left-handed
THE TRIPODERO
When it spies another beast, the tripodero stuns it with a clay pellet from its blow-gun proboscis
THE WHIRLING WHIMPUS

If you are looking for some unusual animals, how about these?

ruining the crops or causing floods. So people who believed in witchcraft also thought that some animals could work magic.

There are animal superstitions about creatures that are just plain ugly, like the toad. There are notions about other animals that are feared by humans, like snakes, wolves, and crocodiles. And there are odd beliefs about animals that appear to work magic. An example of this is the folklore about birds that disappear in the fall and reappear in the spring, when all that has happened is that they have migrated to a warmer climate.

On the less magical side, there are superstitions about using animals to cure diseases. Many people also have believed that they can make themselves beautiful or handsome, get rid of warts, or find their true loves by using animals, parts of animals, or animal products.

Even in modern times, people who claim that they are not the least bit superstitious still believe that certain animals have certain talents. They root for their fierce, frightening animals, like the Detroit Tigers, the University of Michi-

gan Wolverines, or the University of Kentucky Wildcats. They cheer on their sturdy animals, like the Chicago Bears, the University of Colorado Buffaloes, or the University of Connecticut Huskies. They applaud their lightning-swift animals, like the Miami Dolphins, the Toronto Blue Jays, or the South Dakota State University Jackrabbits.

This book is a rundown of many of the unusual ideas and myths that people in various parts of the world have believed about the magic of animals. There are five chapters on the groups of animals with backbones (*vertebrates*) —mammals, birds, reptiles, amphibians, and fish. And there is one chapter devoted to animals without backbones (*invertebrates*), such as spiders and insects.

Probably none of the superstitions in this book are true. But if you are like most people, after you hear about some of them, you will be a little suspicious of your pet dog or cat. And you may never trust a crocodile again!

T.G.A.

CHAPTER 1

Mammals

The mammals are the most highly developed group in the animal kingdom, and human beings belong to this collection of animals with backbones (vertebrates). Mammals have hair and nurse their young with mother's milk. Usually, the young are born alive, after developing inside the body of the mother, not laid in eggs.

Modern mammals vary in size from the tiny shrew, less than two inches long, to the enormous blue whale, over one hundred feet long. Most of the mammals are land animals, although some, like the whale, the porpoise, and the sea cow, live in the sea. The bat is one of the few mammals that is capable of flight.

BADGER

People in the Badger State of Wisconsin don't seem to have superstitions about the animal. But some of the lovesick young men and women there might want to borrow a belief from the West Indies. There is an old voodoo stunt to awaken love. Just bury the foot of a badger under your boy- or girlfriend's bed and he or she will fall in love with you.

BAT

As a furry animal that can fly, the bat is a most unusual creature. And many odd notions have developed about it.

In most places, the bat has a terrible reputation. Because it was thought that the Devil often took the form of a bat, the animal was a symbol of death. In Europe, Asia, and the Americas, it has been said that if a bat flies into the house, someone will die.

But in parts of England, the bat was not a fiend, but a mischievous animal. It was thought that bats stole bacon from farmhouse chimneys. And there are English children who

chant a little rhyme when they see a bat:

Bat, bat, get under my hat
And I'll give you a slice of bacon.

Bat's blood was also used for magical purposes. Most recipes for flying ointment for witches mentioned it as one of the ingredients to help the witch sail around on her broom. And in Central Europe, all a girl has to do to make a boy fall in love with her is to add a few drops of bat's blood to his beer.

If you don't believe that, you will never believe this—a bat can help you become invisible. Just carry the heart of a bat under your right arm. Of if you are in the German Tyrol, wear the left eye of a bat and no one will be able to see you.

In parts of Germany it was believed that if you tied the dried heart of a bat on your arm you would be lucky at cards.

Bats are good weather predictors, too. If you see them flying around the fields at night, there will be good weather.

BEAR

The Norwegian hunters of old drank bears' blood to make them as strong as a bear. But most of the other superstitions about this animal are medical.

For example, there is the famous concoction called bear grease, made from the fat of the creature. In sixteenth-century Europe, it was believed that bear grease would cure baldness. It would also prevent blight in the garden if you rubbed it on your garden tools.

Want to cure a child of whooping cough? Let the patient ride on a bear's back. Of course, unless the bear is gentle, there is a possibility that something worse than whooping cough might happen to the child!

To prevent fits, take some fur from a live bear's belly, boil it in alcohol, and put it on the soles of your feet. If you suffer from backache, sleep on a bearskin.

Bears' teeth come in handy, too. Give one to a baby to gum on and the result will be strong teeth. Carry a bear tooth as a charm and it will prevent toothache.

To some people, the bear was as mysterious an animal as the unicorn. Here is an illustration from a fourteenth-century book showing a fight between the two creatures, with another bear, obviously thirsty, looking on.
Another old drawing of the bear. Since bears took honey from hives, they were often thought to be enemies of the bees. Some called this animal the "bee-wolf."

The cat can be a witch's "familiar." One English witch, who confessed in 1618, said that her mother was also a witch. She saw her mother's familiar, "the cat, Rutterkin, leap on her shoulder and suck her neck."

BEAVER

The Indians of British Columbia in Canada had a superstition about the beaver—rub the body of a baby girl with the body of a beaver. This will make her work harder for her husband when she gets married.

CAT

In the Middle Ages, a cat was often thought to be the Devil himself, or at least a witch's familiar. Also, it was an animal that, it was said, could be a witch in disguise. But a witch could turn into a cat only nine times—matching the supposed nine lives of the cat.

No question about it, the cat is associated with luck. In most places, the cat that brings the worst luck is the black cat. But in parts of England a black cat is lucky, and a white cat brings bad luck. In any case, if a black cat comes into the house, don't chase it outside. You must stroke it gently along the spine or it will take the luck of the house with it.

Sailors and actors are particularly fond of cats. A cat on a ship brings good luck. And it

can be very helpful when there is no wind to drive the sail. Just put the cat under a pot on the deck and a good wind will come up. And don't throw the cat overboard or a terrible storm will occur. Every theater should have a cat. Some actors think that if the cat looks interested while the actors are rehearsing, the play will be a success. But if it runs across the stage during a performance, it is a disaster. Never kick the theater cat or it will bring on a catastrophe.

In some places it is believed that cats creep into cradles to suck the breath from young babies. And these animals seem to have a lot to do with illness. Many used to think they caused sickness and death.

In the seventeenth century, Increase Mather, the New England Puritan minister, wrote, "There are some who, if a cat accidentally comes into a room, though they neither see of it, nor are told of it, will presently be in a sweat and ready to die away." There were even those who believed that if a sick person dreamed of cats or a cat fight, the result would be death.

The cat has been associated with the moon. The moon grows first bigger and then smaller, just like the smile on the Cheshire Cat in Alice in Wonderland, *which looks here like a crescent moon.*

To the Japanese, the cat could be a witch in animal form. This is a painting by the famous Japanese artist Kuniyoshi. It is called "The Cat-Witch."

On the brighter side, there are many superstitions that claim that cats can help sick people. If someone is ill in the house, an old technique tells how to transfer the disease from the human to a cat—douse the cat with the patient's wash water and chase it out of the house.

A dried cat skin put on the face cures toothache. Broth made from a black cat cures consumption. A whole cat boiled in olive oil makes a perfect dressing for wounds.

A stye in the eye could be cured with a cat. Just pull the cat's tail over the affected eye and say:

> *I poke thee. I don't poke thee.*
> *I poke the queff* [stye] *that's under the eye.*
> *O qualyway, O qualyway.*

It was said that this technique could also cure warts and the itch.

Cats are good for predicting the weather. When a cat sneezes, it means rain. When these animals scamper around wildly, there will be a wind. If they wash their ears, it means rain,

and when they sit with their backs to the fire it is a prediction of frost or storms.

In Indonesia, cats can be used to make rain. All that is necessary is for a woman to put a pot upside down on her head. Then she puts it on the ground and fills it with water. Finally, she washes a cat in the water until the animal is half drowned. This causes heavy rains. (But how can she figure out exactly when the cat is half drowned?)

Cats are also associated with romance, especially in the Ozark regions of the United States. There, if a girl accidentally steps on a cat's tail, she will marry within the year. But it must be an accident.

If she can't make up her mind whether to marry a certain man or not, she can use a technique called "leave it to the cat." Take three hairs from a cat's tail and wrap them in a piece of white paper. Put the paper under the doorstep. The next morning, carefully unwrap the paper without disturbing the hairs. Look to see if the hairs spell *Y* for yes, or *N* for no.

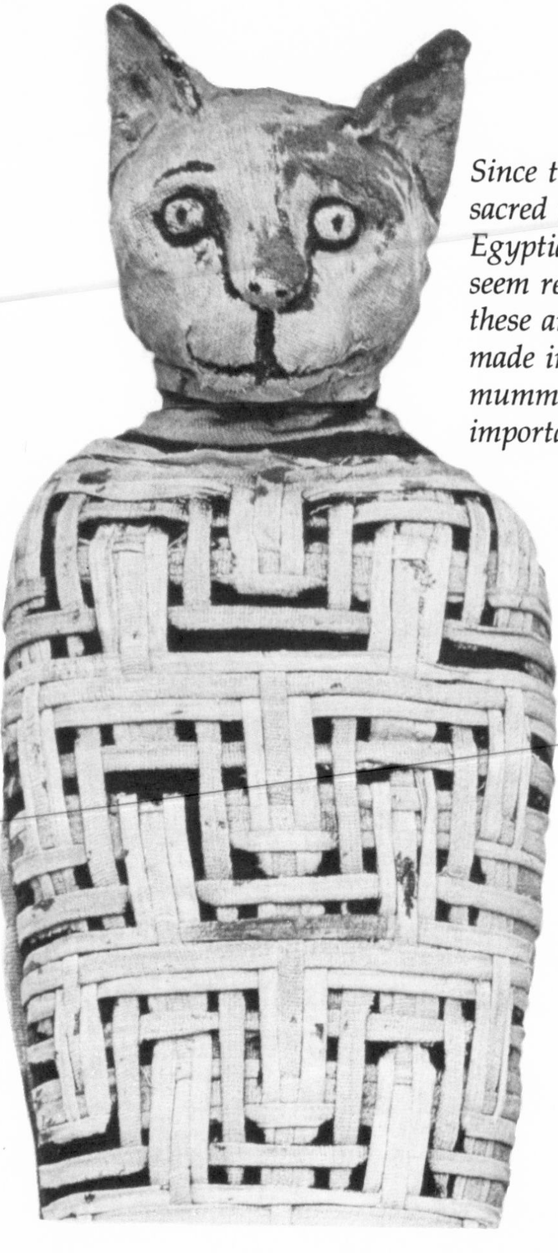

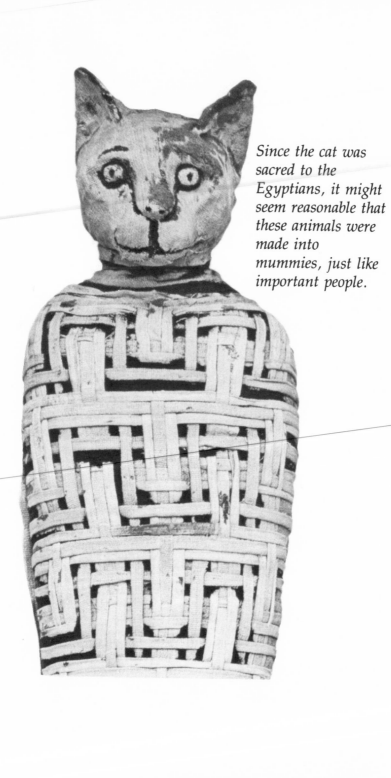

Since the cat was sacred to the Egyptians, it might seem reasonable that these animals were made into mummies, just like important people.

Another Ozark belief was that unmarried women should have a cat handy when they have a quilting bee. Once the quilt is finished, they should toss a cat in it and then release the animal. Whichever woman the cat heads for will be the first one married.

One Ozark warning. If a family keeps black cats, none of the daughters of the house will marry.

Sneezing cats have something to do with romance, too. In many places, if a cat sneezes once near a bride, it means that she will have a good marriage. But if the cat sneezes three or more times it just means that the whole family will catch cold.

Finally, to finish off the cat, here are three unrelated superstitions. Cats are good for hunting mice unless your particular cat was born in May. May cats are only good for killing glowworms and snakes. There is an old Hebrew belief that if you eat what has been nibbled by a cat, you will become forgetful. In the southern part of the United States, never kick a cat. You will get rheumatism.

CATTLE

There is a Hindu idea that concerns the dying. If a person dies while holding onto a cow's tail, it is certain that he or she will be blessed.

In Europe just a little more than a century ago, some people had a strange way of warding off a cattle epidemic. Slaughtered cows' hearts were boiled and stuck full of pins.

A statue of the giant ox of American legend, Babe, with her master, Paul Bunyan.

DOG

Dogs have been favorites of humans for centuries. In ancient Egypt, the city of Cynopolis was named for the dog *Cynos*. A law there required that the people take in all stray dogs. Cynopolis even went to war with a nearby town when someone from that town ate one of its dogs.

The governor of ancient Babylon was a dog lover too. He owned so many dogs that he made four towns exempt from paying taxes as long as the people fed the dogs properly. And there is an old saying in the Ozark Mountains of the United States: "A man who can't make friends with dogs can't be trusted."

Dogs are associated with luck. An old Hebrew superstition claims that if a dog passes between two men, they will have bad luck. And if a dog cannot stop howling, it means that the angel of death is strolling through town.

The Spaniards look on the brighter side. It is lucky there to call dogs by name.

Of course dogs are sometimes associated with medicine. Here is an old Hebrew recipe for curing fever:

Take seven prickles from seven palm trees,
seven chips from seven beams,
seven nails from seven bridges,
seven ashes from seven ovens,
seven scoops of earth from seven door sockets,
seven pieces of pitch from seven ships,
seven handfuls of cumin,
and seven hairs from the beard of an old dog,
and tie them to the neck hole of the shirt
with a white twisted cord.

There was an old Mesopotamian technique to cure a child of a disease by transferring the sickness to a dog. First, put a loaf of bread on the child's head. Next, recite a certain incantation three times. Rub the child with the loaf from head to foot. Finally, feed the bread to a dog. The dog will get the disease, and the child will be cured.

Speaking of disease, there is another ancient Hebrew belief about hydrophobia, or rabies. If you are bitten by a mad dog, don't look in any water that may be nearby. If you were to see the reflection of the animal that bit you, you would surely die of the bite.

Did you ever have any desire to talk to the birds? All you have to do is to cook a dog's and a fox's heart together and eat them. What's more, if you kiss someone after eating the hearts, he or she will be able to talk to the birds, too.

ELEPHANT

In parts of Africa a ring or bracelet made out of braided elephant's hair will bring you good luck.

GOAT

In many places it was believed that a witch could ride off to a grand witches' meeting on a goat. And when the Devil appeared at these witches' meetings, he came in the form of a goat.

In ancient Rome, a she-goat could bring you good luck. If one crossed your path as you were leaving the house it was a sign that something good was going to happen to you.

If you fall down a lot, here is a cure—keep a desert goat's tongue in your pocket at all times.

(Above) In a thirteenth-century manuscript, horses were pictured as the five senses. At the left, all of them are in a row. At the right is sight. It has wings, and notice the eye in front. (Below) From left to right are touch (a horse rearing to paw the ground), hearing, and smell. Who knows what happened to taste?

HORSE

Superstitions about horses have always been with us. The ancient Celtic people kept white horses in sacred groves. The Celts thought that they could predict the future by watching their movements.

Centuries ago, German tribes kept white horses in their temples. When a war was about to start, one of the horses would be led outside. If the animal stepped over the threshold left foot first, the war would be lost. So the fighting was called off.

In parts of India, a specially consecrated horse was allowed to run free for a year. The horse was protected by warriors who made sure the king on whose territory the horse roamed would either pay homage or fight.

In Europe it used to be thought that a horse could be a witch's familiar. A traveling English performing horse was burned as a witch in Rouen, France, because it was so clever that it was thought to be a human in disguise.

Long ago in the Pennsylvania Dutch country of the United States, children were protected

from witchcraft by being passed through a horse collar. And horse-head decorations on the gables of German houses warded off evil spirits.

Horses have one problem. They are susceptible to the evil eye. (The evil eye is supposed to be a way of harming a person just by looking at him or her.) To combat this, many horses were outfitted with fancy tack—brass pieces showing the sun, the moon, or a heart.

Like so many other animals, horses came in handy to amateur doctors. Horse hairs placed around the neck were said to cure goiter. If a child has worms, make him or her eat a horse-hair sandwich. In England, it was thought that cancer could be cured with horse spurs (the callouses on the inside of the horse's leg). Just powder them and drink them in a mixture of warm milk and ale. There is an old Hebrew idea that a horse's blood will cure warts.

In England and our own Ozark regions, it was believed that a dream about a white horse meant there would be sickness or death in the

family. But a dream about a horse of a different color was good luck. Ancient Hebrews didn't agree. White-horse dreams were good, but red-horse dreams were bad. At any rate, if your own horse is having a run of bad luck, just change its name, and that will change its luck.

In parts of the southern United States it is believed that you can't trust a man who rides a red horse. And in the same regions, horses can help you make sure that your wish comes true. When you see a newborn colt, spit in your hand and make the wish. Or you can use the "stamping" technique. Wet your right thumb and press the wet part into your left palm. Then "stamp" a mule with the left palm. After twenty different mules, your wish will be granted. You can stamp white horses, too, but it takes one hundred of them to do the job.

HYENA

Hyenas were thought to be truly magic animals, probably because of their cry, which sounds so much like human laughter. The Arabs believed that if a hyena steps on your

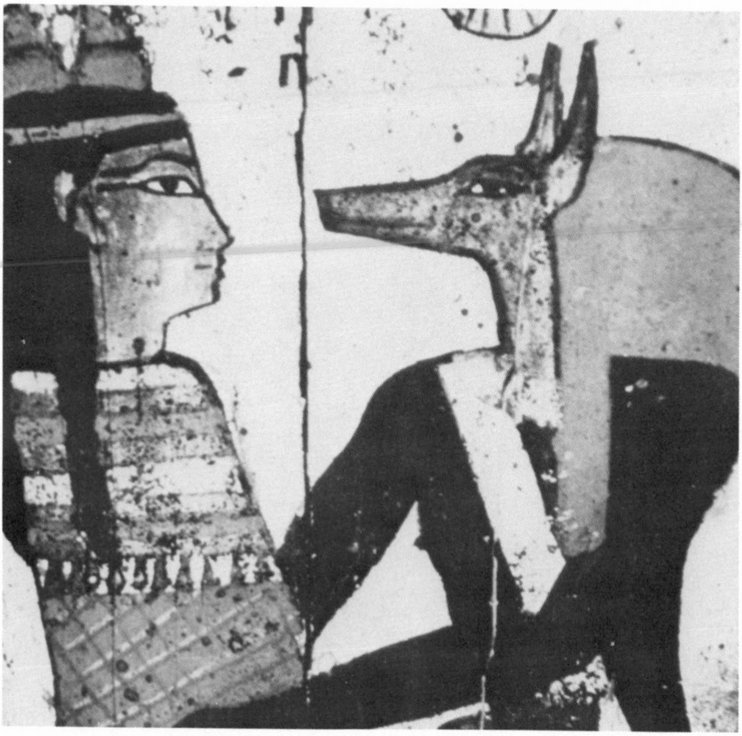

The hyena's cousin, the jackal, was associated with death. Here is an ancient wall painting showing the Egyptian jackal-headed god, Anubis, whose job was to guide the dead to the place of judgment.

shadow, you will lose the powers of speech and movement. And if your pet dog is on the roof and casts a shadow on the ground, the hyena has but to step on the shadow, and the dog will fall off the roof. What it was doing there in the first place is anyone's guess!

A hyena tooth worn around the neck, according to the ancient Greeks, will protect you from both witches and night animals. To accomplish the same thing, smear hyena's blood on the doorposts of your house. Hyena skin hung on the gate of an English orchard wards off hail and lightning.

Hyenas, according to the old Greeks, can help a man in love. Just touch the lips of your girlfriend with a hyena's whisker, and she will be yours forever.

Some primitive Australian tribes believed that if you wore the heart of a hyena you would become cowardly. But who would want such a piece of jewelry?

LION

The lion has often been thought of as a symbol of strength. East African Masai warriors would drink the blood of this animal to make them strong. But that didn't necessarily mean that all these people thought that the lion was brave. There were tales told that the lion was afraid of the crowing of a rooster.

Some thought that a sick lion could be cured with the blood of an ape. And, by the way, clothing wrapped in a lion's skin was supposed to be safe from moths.

In this scene from an Indian temple, the job of a lion is to pull the planet Saturn through the sky on a cart.

MOLE

There is an ancient Hebrew love charm that might come in handy. If a woman wants a man to fall in love with her, all she has to do is find a male mole and hit it on its right foot. The same thing works for men, with a female mole.

PIG

For centuries, the pig has been either loved or hated by human beings. It is a staple food for some, forbidden to others.

The pig, like the horse, is said to be vulnerable to the evil eye. But the animal does have talent. It is a weather prophet, since it is believed by some to be able to smell or see the wind. In parts of the United States, it is supposed to know when a tornado is coming. But never mention a pig to a sailor or it will bring bad luck.

There was an old Irish custom that had to do with pigs. A pig in the house brings bad luck except on the first of May. On that day, welcome the animal in and you will have good luck.

The wild boar is a symbol of death and destruction.

PORPOISE

It is said that if a sailor finds a dead porpoise at sea, he will have good luck.

RABBIT

Everyone knows that a rabbit's foot is a good-luck charm. In the southern part of England, it can also be used as a love charm to bring back the affections of a lost love.

Rabbits can bring good luck in other ways,

In the old Aesop fable the rabbit and the hare are not known for cleverness. Illustration by Arthur Rackham.

too. On the first day of a new moon, go outside and shout "rabbits" or "white rabbits" the first thing in the morning. This should be done before you say anything else that morning. Some people say that you have to go outside and shout "black rabbits" the night before. And that should be the last thing you say that evening. Good luck will be with you.

And in Delaware, if you recite a rabbit chant first thing on the first day of the month, good luck will be yours for the whole month. If you remember to say it on New Year's Day, you will have good luck for the entire year. Just say:

Rabbit, rabbit, bring me luck
For this is the first of ______!

In England, a rabbit running down the village street is thought by some to be a warning of fire.

Rabbits crossing your path mean various things. If one crosses from left to right, you will have bad luck. But you can get rid of the bad luck if you tear your clothing a little. If you are a fisherman and a rabbit crosses your path, you

might as well give up. You won't catch any fish that day. If a rabbit crosses the path of a pregnant woman, she should tear a piece of cloth from her dress and burn it. Otherwise, her child is supposed to be born with a harelip.

Finally, a rabbit's foot is said to cure both colic and rheumatism.

In Lapland, reindeer were sacrificial animals. Their blood was used on sacred objects and for medicinal purposes. An illustration from a book published in 1555.

A pair of strange-looking seals, probably drawn by someone who had never seen the animal. They come from a book written in the 1700s.

SEAL

According to the folklore of some Eskimos, if a man kills a seal he must make atonement as if he were a murderer. He is forbidden to scrape frost from a window. He can't clean drips from his lamp. And he also can't shake his bed, scrape hair from skins, and work in wood, stone, or ivory.

If a woman kills a seal, she is forbidden to comb her hair or wash her face.

SHEEP

Sheep can be lucky or unlucky for you. In England and Germany it is considered good luck to meet a flock as you leave your house in the morning. And when you see your first new lamb in the spring, it is good luck if its head is turned away from you. But if a German sheep bears three black lambs, someone in the family will die.

The ancient Scots had a way of predicting the future with a sheep's bone. They would take a "speal bone"—the blade bone of a shoulder of mutton—and make a prediction based upon the lines they found on it.

Sheep can also help the lovelorn. In England it was said that a girl could get back a faithless lover by sticking a knife in a sheep's shoulder blade and saying:

It's not this bone I wish to stick
But (so-and-so's) heart I wish to prick.
Whether he be asleep or awake
I'll have him come to me and speak.

An unmarried woman can go to the sheep

A thirteenth-century Persian astrological painting. Mars is in Aries (the ram) and in conjunction with Jupiter. The figures below are, from left to right: Jupiter, Mars, Venus, Mercury, and Saturn.

stall at night on Christmas Eve and grab an animal in the dark. If it is a male sheep, she will be married during the coming year. If it is a female, she will have to wait until the next Christmas Eve and try again.

Sheep come in handy in problem medical cases, too. Less than one hundred years ago,

there were cases in Devonshire, England, where people thought that their illnesses had been caused by witchcraft. One cure was to stick pins in a sheep heart and recite:

May each pin
Thus stuck in
This poor heart
In hers go
Who hurts me so
Till she departs.

Want a cure for whooping cough? Take the afflicted child to the sheep stall at dawn and let a sheep breathe on him or her. Then push the sheep away and put the child down on the ground where the sheep has been lying.

SKUNK

This animal is an important one in the Ozark regions of the United States. Folklore there says that skunk oil made from the fat of the skunk when it is trapped in winter can cure throat ailments. On the other hand, the smell might be able to cure anything!

SQUIRREL

Some Navaho Indians used to tie a squirrel's tail to a cradle to protect the baby.

WEASEL

There were Indian tribes who thought that if you ate the heart of a weasel you could predict the future.

Gef, the name of a ghostly weasel that haunted a farmhouse on the Isle of Man in the Irish Sea, it is said. Not only could he imitate several animals, but he learned to talk.

Wolves have often meant evil doings. Here is a black wolf serving as transportation for the demon Andras, who is responsible for stirring up quarrels.

WOLF

The wolf has been respected and feared for centuries. Even the ancient Romans thought that this animal had some magical powers. If you see a wolf running to your right with its mouth full, you will have good luck. On the other hand, if a wolf came into a Roman army camp, it had to be killed. If it escaped, the army was sure to be defeated.

In some countries a wolf's head was nailed to the door for protection against witches and their charms. And there are those who believed that if you were robbed, all you had to do was put a wolf's tooth under your pillow. You would see the thief in your dreams.

CHAPTER 2

Birds

Birds come in all shapes and sizes, from the male bee hummingbird, which is smaller than the female, whose wingspan is less than two inches, to the wandering albatross, whose wingspan can reach over eleven feet. The largest flightless bird is the North African ostrich, which can be nine feet tall and weigh over three hundred pounds.

Birds are backboned animals whose bodies are covered with feathers. They have light, air-filled bones, and most of them can fly. They have no teeth, and they lay eggs.

There are a few superstitions about birds in general. A bird that comes into a house is an

The ancient Egyptians thought of the air as a human-headed bird that went along with the dead to the underworld.

example. In the United States, there is a belief that if the bird is white, bad luck will follow. A bird of any other color in the house brings good luck.

This same belief is found in Malaya, but people there have a cure for the white bird's bad luck—you catch the bird and smear it with oil, then let it go outside. It will fly away, taking the bad luck with it.

An old Hebrew cure for headache goes like this. Wrap a thread three times around your head. Next, take the thread off and hang the loop in a tree. If a bird flies through the loop, the headache will go away.

Finally, here is a cure for hepatitis. Stare into the eyes of any yellow-eyed bird, and the disease will be transferred to the animal.

BUZZARD

In the Ozark mountains, you can make a wish when you see a flying buzzard. If the bird doesn't flap its wings while you are wishing, your wish will be granted.

CARDINAL

People in the Ozarks seem to relate this bird to kissing. If a cardinal flies across a girl's path, she will be kissed twice before nightfall. And if a girl sees a cardinal perched on a branch or a fence, she must start blowing kisses to it and make a wish. If the bird flies away before she gets to the third blown kiss, her wish will come true. If she gets past three kisses, it's no good.

CHICKEN

Chickens are the most numerous birds in the world. They have been domesticated for centuries and so almost everyone in the world is familiar with them. No wonder that so many superstitions have arisen about them.

Chickens were used by the ancient Romans to predict the future through a technique called *alectryomancy* or *alectormancy*. This was a method of predicting the future using a rooster.

First draw a circle on the ground and divide it up into sections—one section for each letter of the alphabet, or twenty-six in the case of English. (Many other languages have more or fewer letters in their alphabets. Spanish has 28, for example.) Label each section for a different letter and put a grain of corn or wheat in each.

Next, get a white rooster and cut off his toenails. Say a few incantations and put him in the middle of the circle. More verses follow, and then you watch which grain he picks up. Each time he eats one, replace it. In this way the rooster will spell out the message.

It is said that this method was used to predict

which person would replace the Roman emperor Valens Caesar. But the rooster ate only four grains, spelling the word *Theo.* The problem was that no one knew whether he was choosing Theodosius, Theodotus, Theodorus, or Theodectes. Theodosius was the eventual ruler.

A hen can be used to get back property in Hungary. If you are robbed, take a black hen into a room with you. Both of you must then go without food all day for nine successive Fridays. During that time, the thief will have to return his loot or he will die.

The crowing of a rooster has always had its share of superstitious lore connected with it. All over the world, people have believed that the cock's crowing at dawn is lucky. The noise drives away all the evil night things. But there are exceptions.

Some have thought that if a rooster crows three times, someone in the house will die. But this can be prevented. If you want him to stop crowing, rub his head with olive oil, and put a garland of vines around his neck.

There are places in the United States where it is believed that if a rooster crows on a porch, there will be a visitor to the house. If he crows facing the house, at the front door, or facing a banister, there will be a death in the house.

Crowing roosters can influence the weather, too. If a cock crows while it is raining, the rain will stop. And there is an old Ozark rhyme that indicates the rooster can cause rain:

If a cock crows when he goes to bed,
He'll get up with a wet head.

There are other ways that the rooster can make it rain. In Germany, you can throw a rooster into the air to cause thunder and lightning. During the Middle Ages, some Germans tried to bring rain by killing a white rooster, then filling its body with myrrh, white pepper, frankincense, milk, and wine. The next step was to hold it up toward the sun and recite an incantation.

Some Germans believed that every seven years a rooster could lay one egg. If you were lucky enough to find that magic egg, you threw

In the old days, witches were thought to cook up a rainstorm by using a rooster. In this old print, it looks as if they have been successful.

it over your house—to prevent thunderstorms.

There were those who thought that you could become invisible if you carried the heart of a black hen under your right arm. And an old Hebrew superstition says that a rooster should be killed if he upsets a dish. This clumsiness meant that he was possessed by demons. Ancient Romans thought that a locked door could be opened by using the tail feathers of a rooster instead of a key.

Chickens can come in handy in curing diseases. In Scotland, burying a rooster in the dirt floor under the bed of someone with epilepsy will cure the illness. In Germany, hiding the head, heart, and right foot of a rooster in a house will ward off all illnesses. In the Ozarks, if a black hen and her chicks walk over the body of a child who has chicken pox, the child will be cured.

An old Hebrew belief says that if a dying person is lying on a feather bed containing chicken feathers, it is better to move the patient. The feathers will prolong the death pains.

Chickens have cosmetic functions in the Ozarks. Freckles can be removed by putting chicken blood on your face. And if a girl wants to be beautiful, all she has to do is eat a raw chicken heart.

When it comes time to be married, an old Hebrew superstition says that the bride and groom will have good luck if a hen and rooster are tossed over the couple. In parts of Germany, it is the worst kind of luck if a wedding party on the way to the church comes across two roosters fighting.

Finally, in the Ozarks it is very bad luck to dream of chickens.

CROW

The cawing of a crow has been thought of as evil for centuries. To some people, having noisy crows fly over their houses in the evening meant death. On the other hand, these birds could be useful. In ancient Rome, if you wanted to scare away demons, all you had to do was to kick a crow in the morning.

The ancient Hebrews had a way of using a

crow to unlock a door. Just smear the right foot of a male crow with the fat of a snake and rub the lock with it. In Czechoslovakia, if you ate three crow's hearts, you would become a crack shot. In ancient Greece, if you ate three crow's hearts raw, you would be able to predict the future.

Also in ancient Greece, if you wanted to touch up your gray hair, you would wash it in crows' eggs. It was then supposed to turn black. But there was a warning. While you were washing your hair, your mouth had to be filled with oil or else your teeth would turn black, too.

Crows can be used for prediction. In the Ozarks, if two crows are circling over a cabin, any unmarried woman inside will find a husband. In parts of England, if a crow is perched on a dead tree branch, it will rain before night. But if it perches on a live branch, the day will be fine.

In the Ozarks, there is a little verse to recite when you see crows flying together:

One's unlucky,
Two's lucky,
Three's health,
Four's wealth,
Five's sickness,
Six is death.

In Babylonia, it was thought that if you catch a crow and then let it go, it will fly away with your fever. But to dream of a crow cawing means that you will have sadness in your life. Finally, if you don't put on something new for Easter, you will find crow droppings on your clothes.

CUCKOO

The ancient Greeks believed that the cuckoo turned into a hawk during the winter. Most of the other superstitions about this bird have to do with its song.

Let's take the cry of the first cuckoo in the spring. In England and Scotland, it was believed that you could tell how many more years you would live by counting the times that the

cuckoo called. And an unmarried woman could tell how many years she would remain unwed. This was also true in Germany, but there it was felt that if the cuckoo called more than ten times it must be insane, and so was unreliable.

There were places where you were supposed

In this illustration from an old book, Merry Tales of the Madmen of Gotam, *a cuckoo is talking to a man.*

to wish for something when you heard the first cuckoo. And if you had money in your pocket at the time, you would have money all year.

In England, if by accident you heard the first cuckoo while you were in bed, someone in the family would get sick. If this happened in Scotland, it was just bad luck. But in France, the hearer would turn into a lazy idler.

Fishermen should be careful. If they hear the cuckoo call first thing in the morning, they will catch no fish. On the other hand, the cuckoo's call can cure disease. In Germany, if you roll on the grass when you hear it, you won't get lumbago. And in England, scrape up the dirt from beneath your right foot and you will be cured of fleas.

An unmarried man can use the bird's song to help him find a wife. He looks under his left shoe (when he hears the cuckoo) and finds a hair of the same color as that of his future wife.

The Danes believed that the cuckoo, a bird that uses other birds' nests, was so busy giving clues to people that it had no time to build a nest of its own.

The eagle is a symbol of power and leadership. Our national bird as a United States emblem.

EAGLE

Various parts of the eagle are supposed to have great powers. Mix its feathers with a special herb, cook it, and eat it, and it will cure madness. The eagle liver mixed with honey and balsam cures cataracts. And its heart is a love charm.

The Pawnee Indians made an object called a storm eagle. This was a dead eagle stuffed with magical objects that could raise a storm.

(Facing page) Doves were thought to be symbols of love. Here is Venus, the Roman goddess of love, riding in a dove-drawn chariot.

GOOSE

In England, if you eat goose on September 29, Michaelmas Day, you will be lucky. There is an old saying, "If you eat goose at Michaelmas Day you will never want for money all the year round." And in Yorkshire, in northern England, you can predict the weather with a goose. If the breastbone is dark, there will be a severe winter. If it is light, the winter will be mild.

HAWK

A hawk seen flying from your right to your left means bad luck in sections of America.

HUMMINGBIRD

A voodoo recipe in Haiti tells how a man can win the heart of a woman. He makes a powder of dried hummingbird flesh and herbs and blows it on her.

LAPWING

In the Middle Ages it was thought that if a man would hang the heart, eye, or brain of a

A drawing from India of the god Brahma, riding on a magic goose.

lapwing around his neck, he would improve his intelligence and his memory. And if he couldn't find a lapwing, a black plover would do.

MAGPIE

People in Shropshire, England, once thought that if they saw a magpie flying from their right to their left, it meant bad luck. They would also make a wish when they saw their first magpie in the spring.

Almost everywhere in Britain it was felt that killing a magpie brought terribly bad luck. And in Wales, you should tip your hat to this bird when you see it.

In southern Germany it was thought that if a magpie sings near your house it means disaster. But if it merely chatters, a guest will soon arrive.

When magpies fly together, you can predict the future with this little poem:

One for sorrow, two for mirth,
Three for a wedding, four for a birth.

Or with this one:

One for sorrow, two for joy,
Three for a girl, four for a boy.

MOCKINGBIRD

There is an Ozark legend that if a woman hears a mockingbird at night, she must put on a man's hat. That will ensure a happy marriage.

NIGHTINGALE

This bird is famous for nonstop singing, so if you put a nightingale's eyes and heart next to a person in bed, they will keep him or her awake. Going one step further, grind up the eyes and heart and mix them in someone's drink. Then he or she will die of insomnia.

OWL

Owls have been associated with witchcraft for centuries. Many of them have almost human faces and horrible cries that frighten the superstitious.

In the Ozark mountains, the owl is some-

In this drawing by the Spanish artist Francisco Goya, many of the common elements of witchcraft are shown—two ugly old crones, a flying broomstick, and an owl.

times called the "witch chicken," and is thought to be able to charm chickens off their perches. But if you nail part of a great horned owl over your door, it will keep away witches. In parts of Asia, you can place a dead owl over a child's bed to frighten away evil spirits.

These birds can be helpful in other ways. In

A drawing of an owl painted on a coffin in Egypt almost four thousand years ago. It was a symbol of death and mourning.

India, there was a belief that if you put owl feathers under a child's pillow, they would put the child to sleep. The ancient Greeks had a belief that if you put an owl's heart on a woman's breast it would force her to tell the truth. And gray hair would turn to black if you washed it with owl's eggs.

Owl-egg soup cured epilepsy, but only if it was made from an egg containing a male owl.

PEACOCK

The peacock comes in handy when you want to predict the weather. It is supposed to dance and utter cries when a storm is approaching.

It was also believed that peacock's bile and blood was a cure for poisoning. And in parts of India, you can burn the feathers of the bird if you suspect that you have been poisoned.

The cry of the peacock is also thought to attract snakes, which the bird then kills. And its feathers are supposed to ward off evil, so some people make umbrellas out of them.

English actors believe that any play with the word "peacock" in it will be a flop.

This is an old drawing of a pelican, from the time it was thought that the bird fed her young with her own blood.

ROBIN

The European robin is usually looked on as a lucky bird. In parts of Germany, it is supposed to protect houses from lightning. Also, if a bridal couple see a robin on the way from their wedding ceremony, they will be lucky.

As you might expect, it is not a good idea to harm a robin. In England, Scotland, and Germany, if you kill one, your cows will give bloody milk. In parts of England and Bohemia, if you rob a robin's nest, your hands will tremble. In Wales, if you do the same, you will break an arm or a leg.

Robins can help predict the weather:

If the robin sings in the bush,
Then the weather will be coarse;
But if the robin sings on the barn,
Then the weather will be warm.

SEAGULL

On parts of the English coast, seagulls are believed to be the souls of drowned sailors.

STARLING

There is an old Hebrew superstition that says a guest will arrive at your home if a starling sings at night.

STORK

According to legends, storks are almost human. They weep human tears when they are wounded. The male stork kills his mate if she is unfaithful. Young storks care for their parents in their old age.

They also are responsible for bringing luck. A stork's nest on a building will protect it from fire—but if you steal the stork's young from the nest, the building will burn down. When a stork lights on a house in some places, it is believed that a wedding will take place. But in other places, this means bad luck.

The idea of the stork bringing babies originated in Germany. Baby boys with good dispositions ride on its back, and naughty boy babies are carried in its bill.

When a stork appears in late spring, it helps

forecast the weather. If it is a white stork, there will be dry weather. If it is black, there will be rain.

Storks' stomachs will cure diseases in cattle. And if you use stork sinews to bind up your foot, it will cure gout.

All in all, the stork is a highly prized bird. Some of them even kill snakes. So in ancient Thessaly, in eastern Greece, a man who killed a stork was considered to be a murderer.

SWALLOW

In many places, the swallow is thought to cause spring to arrive. We have a saying that "one swallow does not a summer make," but as far back as the second century, boys on the Greek Islands were going from house to house in the spring, singing:

The swallow is here and
a new year he brings,
As he lengthens the days
with the beats of his wings,

White and black
Are his belly and back.
Pay his tribute once more
With cheese in his basket
And pork from your store,
And wine from its flasket,
And eggs from your casket,
And bread when we ask it.

In the Ozarks, to have swallows nesting in your barn meant that the building would never be struck by lightning. In Europe, if you found a stone inside a swallow, it would cheer you up.

But there were ways that this bird could cause bad luck. In Greece, a swallow fluttering around your head signaled misfortune. In France and Hungary, if a swallow flies under a cow's belly the result will be bloody milk. In Yorkshire, England, to have a swallow fly down a chimney means a death in the family.

If you are nasty to a swallow, you will be repaid in kind. In the Tyrol, in Germany, if you destroy a swallow's nest, your own home will

burn down. In France, if you steal the bird's eggs from its nest, your horse will go lame.

These birds can also be used for weather predicting. In England, when the swallows fly low, there will be bad weather. And the Chinese used to throw swallows into a pond to make it rain.

There were people who thought that the human soul might leave the body in the form of a swallow. Here is an Egyptian drawing of the soul of a scribe, painted somewhere around 1250 B.C.

If you tie a swallow's crop in a yellow cloth and tie it around your neck, it will cure a fever. But you can also fight the fever with mud from its nest. And various parts of these birds were supposed to cure snake bite, epilepsy, and even rabies.

They could also be used to predict marriage. In Czechoslovakia, if an unmarried woman first saw a single swallow in the spring, she would be married within the year. If there were two birds together, she would remain single.

SWAN

There is an old story going back to the ancient Greeks that a swan sings as it dies. That created so much sympathy for this bird that to kill one in Siberia or Ireland meant death to the killer.

TURTLEDOVE

In ancient Syria, to touch one of these birds was bad luck. Nowadays, there are many superstitions about the turtledove to be found in the Ozark Mountains.

There, to dream of the turtledove brings

good luck. When you hear the first turtledove in the spring, make a wish, turn around three times on your left heel, and take off your left shoe. If you find a hair in the shoe that is the same color as your wife's, husband's, or sweetheart's, the wish will be granted.

Unmarried women can do something similar to find out who they will marry. When the first turtledove calls in the spring, take off your right stocking. Inside will be a hair the same color as the hair of your future husband.

If you are a desperate unmarried man, you can also use a turtledove. Just hide the dried tongue of this bird in your girlfriend's house and she will fall in love with you.

WHIP-POOR-WILL

In the Ozarks, if you are unmarried and hear a whip-poor-will, cross your fingers, then count the cries. That is the number of years you must wait to be married.

(Facing page) A drawing by Francisco Goya shows blood-sucking vultures as emblems of war.

WOODPECKER

In England, the cry of the green woodpecker means that it will rain soon. And among the Masai tribe in Africa, the sound means luck of one sort or another. If the cry of a gray woodpecker comes from the right, it means good luck. If from the left, it means bad luck. If it comes from behind you and you are traveling to another town, you will get a good reception.

CHAPTER 3

Reptiles

Turtles, tortoises, lizards, snakes, alligators, crocodiles, and a few other animals belong to the group called reptiles. These animals usually have scales on their dry-skinned bodies. If they have feet, they also have claws. They lay eggs and are cold-blooded. That means that their body temperatures change with the changes in temperature of their environment.

Reptiles can be large, like the salt-water crocodile of Southeast Asia. The largest specimen of this animal ever seen was thirty-three feet long and weighed three and one-half tons. The smallest reptile is a type of gecko found

This seagoing reptile monster was supposed to have been seen off the coast of Galveston, Texas.

only on the island of Virgin Gordo in the British Virgin Islands. One specimen was less than three-quarters of an inch long.

CROCODILE

In ancient Egypt, where many people were lost to crocodiles every year, the animal was looked upon as being magical and was even regarded as an evil god. But there was a way to escape the creature by using an incantation. In this

verse, Mako is a mystic crocodile, Set is a god, and Ra is man:

Stop, crocodile Mako, son of Set!
Do not wave thy tail;
Do not work thy two arms;
Do not open thy mouth.
May water become as a burning fire before thee!
The spear of the seventy-seven gods is on thine eyes:
The arm of the seventy-seven gods is on thine eye:
Thou who wast fastened with metal claws to the bark of Ra,
Stop, crocodile Mako, son of Set!

LIZARD

Lizards, it is believed in many places, can cause bad luck. On the Malay Peninsula, it was thought that if an iguana (or a tortoise or a snake, for that matter) came into the house, misfortune would come with it. But the problem could be solved if the lizard could be caught and sprinkled with ashes.

In England, it is very bad luck if a lizard

crosses the path of a bride on her way to her wedding. And in Australia, some tribes believed that if anyone killed a lizard, the sky would fall. Green lizards, according to a superstition in Brittany, a section of France, can kill cows by biting them on the nose.

On the other hand, in ancient Assyria, a two-tailed lizard could come in handy to a murderer. If such an animal were cooked in oil and the oil then used to anoint the man he wanted to kill, the man would die.

There were parts of France and Germany where burying a dead lizard under the threshold of the house would scare away witches. And in England, they were thought to be protective of humans. If a lizard saw a snake approaching a sleeping man, it would wake him up to warn him.

The medicinal values of lizards are strange, too. On the island of Madagascar, bury a lizard alive and it will cure your fever. And in England during the Middle Ages, if you suffered from sores, you could lick a lizard first

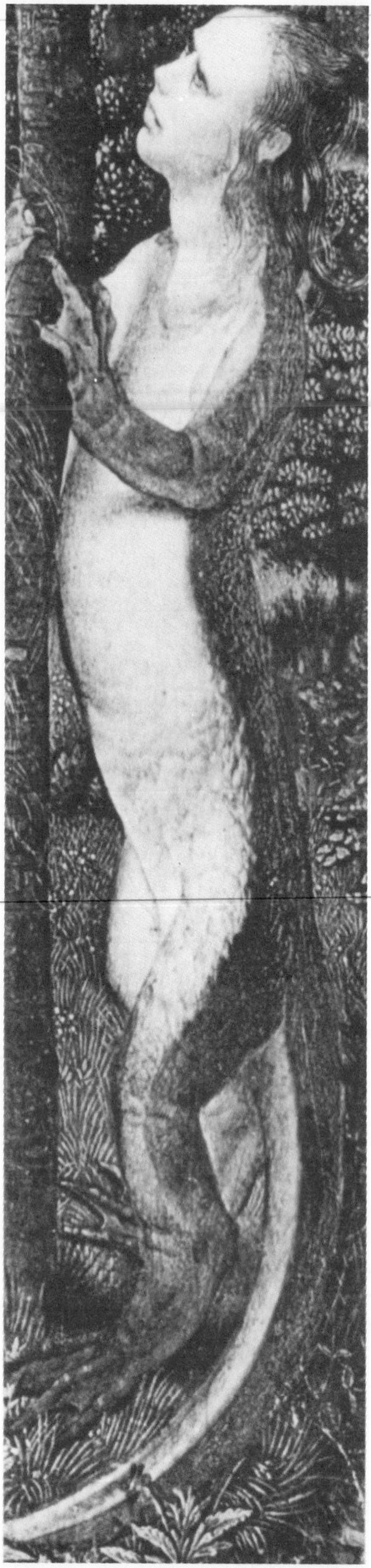

In this painting by the Dutch artist Van der Goes, Eve is being tempted in the Garden of Eden not by a snake, but by a human-headed lizard.

and then lick your sores. That was supposed to be an instant cure.

It is said that every Easter Eve, gypsies in southern Europe would put a dried-up dead lizard in a pot. Then the pot would be carried from tent to tent and each person would spit into it. Finally, the pot and the lizard would be thrown into the lake or the river. This was supposed to banish all illnesses from the tribe for a year.

SNAKE

In many cultures, snakes have been the symbol of evil since the dawn of time. There is a superstition in parts of England that if a live adder appears on your doorstep there will be a death in the family. And if a pregnant woman is frightened by a snake, her baby will be born with a snake neck.

In other parts of England, a dried snakeskin hung over the fireplace not only protects the house from fire, but also is thought to be a general good luck charm.

Snakes can serve as protection, too. There is

an old Hebrew belief about poisoning, for example. If you think that you are about to be poisoned, take a knife that has a snake-bone handle and stick it into your table. If there is any poison around, the knife is supposed to quiver.

Here is a protective snake belief from northern Nigeria:

Cut off the head of a snake and in it plant the seed of the swamp dock. Bury the head in a grave, which must be seven days old. Pour water on it for three consecutive nights. When the plant has grown to a height of three or four feet, go again to the graveyard and strip naked. Pull up the swamp dock and use it as a girdle. If anyone attempts to attack you, the girdle will become a snake that will bite your enemy.

In the Ozarks, there is a superstition that if you dream of a snake, you will get into a fight. Also, if two snakes come into the house at the same time, there will be a wedding.

Like so many other animals, snakes have their medical uses. In some parts of the United States it was believed that if you ground up a

rattlesnake's rattle and put it into the drink of a pregnant woman, it would ease the pains of childbirth. And wrapping a snakeskin around an aching joint would ease the pain of rheumatism. In the United States this has to be a rattlesnake skin; in England it should be an adder skin.

A reptile hoax. This monster skeleton was created by "Doctor" Albert Koch in the 1840s out of a collection of old bones.

CHAPTER 4

Amphibians

The group called the amphibians contains such animals as frogs, toads, and salamanders. Their bodies are covered by a thin, flexible skin, usually moist. And they don't have scales, fur, or feathers. These animals have webbed feet, if they have feet at all, and their toes are usually webbed.

Amphibians lead a double life. Most of them begin life as water-dwelling larvae (like the tadpole). When they are mature (like the frog), they live mainly on land. Often, the baby forms eat plant material and the adults eat animal material, such as insects.

Two old pictures that show the toad's connection with witchcraft. Above, two toads are dancing at a sabbat, *and below, a toad is flying to a sabbat on the back of a skeleton.*

The largest amphibian is probably a giant salamander found in Japan and parts of China. One specimen was found that was five feet long and weighed eighty-eight pounds. The smallest seems to be a type of frog found in Cuba that is about one-half inch long.

FROG

If you want to become invisible, carry the heart of a frog under your right arm.

Frogs have been thought to have something to do with the weather for centuries. In parts of India and South America, for example, special rain frogs were kept in cages. During a drought, these animals were beaten to death to make it rain. There is a similar Hindu belief, but it is less cruel. If you want to make it rain, just pour water over a frog.

The ancient Romans used frogs to protect their crops from storms. First they would drag a frog around the fields. Then they would bury it in the center of the field before they planted the crops. Just before the harvest, they would dig up the frog.

Frogs have their medical uses, too. If either of your eyes is inflamed, hang a frog's eye around your neck, the left or the right, depending on which of your eyes you're trying to cure.

There are two ways of using a frog to cure toothaches, and both of them go back to the ancient Romans. The first one tells you to boil a frog in a mixture of water and vinegar and then hold it in your mouth. The second one is easier—spit in a frog's mouth and tell the animal to take away the pain.

Powdered frog's liver is thought to cure epilepsy. And to cure a fever, swallow a frog's eye that has been plucked out before sunrise.

There were primitive Slavic tribes who thought that frogs, not storks, brought babies.

Frogs were the staff of life to strange creatures in England and France. These were the earliest kinds of fairies, called *Portunes* in England and *Neptunes* in France. They were only a few inches high, with faces wrinkled like little old men's. Their habit was to come into houses at night to roast frogs in front of the fire.

A group of fairies dancing around a little girl in bed. The ugly ones look suspiciously like Portunes or Neptunes.

TOAD

Toads have a reputation for being a part of witchcraft. In twelfth-century France, it was thought that the Devil often appeared as a toad, and had to be kissed. And toads were believed to be witches' familiars, or even the witches themselves. Also, a witch could mix toad spittle with sow-thistle sap and make herself invisible by drinking the brew.

Some ancient Greeks thought that you could kill a man by mixing toad's blood in his wine.

In Romania, no one picked on a toad. It was thought that if you harmed a toad you were capable of killing your own mother. And no one wanted that kind of reputation!

In parts of England, there was an idea that there were men called *toadmen.* They looked like normal human beings, but they had the power to make horses stand still no matter what. And they could also make the same horses excited whenever they wanted to.

They got their power either by skinning a toad or by pegging its body to an anthill until its bones were picked clean. Then they carried

the bones in their pockets until they were dry. At midnight, under a full moon, they floated the bones on a stream. If one bone started to float upstream, it had to be grabbed and saved. That was the magic charm for becoming a toadman.

In the Ozarks, if a toad is seen on a pathway right after a wedding, it means good luck.

Toads are supposed to be able to hear distant thunder. So just watch toads, and if they start to head for the water, it means that they have heard the far-off storm.

Gardeners in England sometimes find that toads come in handy. They drag a toad's body around their gardens before they plant any seeds. Then they bury the body in an earthenware pot in the center of the flowerbed. This is supposed to prevent any creeping thing from injuring the flowers. But if the planting is for vegetables, it is best to dig up the pot right after seeding. If you don't, the food will taste bitter. Oddly enough, some ancient Greeks thought that that very same procedure would prevent storms.

During the Middle Ages, some people thought that there was a magic jewel to be found in the head of a toad. Even Shakespeare wrote of it. In *As You Like It,* the Duke says:

Sweet are the uses of adversity;
Which, like the toad, ugly and venomous,
Wears yet a precious jewel in his head.

This stone was called a *borax* or a *stelon,* and if you made it into a ring, it was supposed to protect you from being poisoned.

A sorcerer removing the precious stone from the head of a toad.

CHAPTER 5

Fish

The fish group of animals contains those water-living, streamlined animals that have scales, fins, and gills. It not only includes the bony fishes, such as bass and trout, but also sharks, rays, and eels.

Probably the largest fish in the sea is the whale shark. One of them was found to be fifty-three feet long and seventy thousand pounds in weight. The smallest fish seems to be a goby fish, found in streams and lakes in the Philippines. It is about two-fifths of an inch long and weighs only 0.0002 of an ounce.

EEL

There is a superstition that if you eat the heart of an eel while it is still warm, you will be able to predict the future. Also, an eel can be used to bring the dead to life, it is thought. As soon as someone dies, take an eel out of the water and allow it to die. Put the body in a mixture of vinegar and vulture's blood. Then bury the body of the eel and the dead person will come back to life.

BONY FISH

In the Ozarks, there is a superstition that if you dream of a fish, you will get rich. And in Wales, trout were used to predict the future. These were special trout, and two of them were kept in special wells. All you had to do was throw bread into the wells. If the trout came up to eat the bread, you would have good luck. If not, too bad.

(Facing page) Here is a collection of animals that could be the familiars of the witch in the drawing. As you can see, fish were thought to be candidates for witchcraft.

Fish have been reported as falling from the sky. This is an eighteenth-century drawing of a fish shower.

People in Western Europe used to think that both mackerel and herring must always be eaten from the tail to the head. If they were eaten from head to tail, the schools of fish in the sea would turn tail and there would be none to eat.

In various places, it was believed that herring could help a person find out who his or her mate would be; if you eat a raw herring you will have a vision of your future spouse. Others believe that if you eat a salted herring on Hallowe'en and go to bed you will dream of your future husband or wife. The herring will have made you thirsty and he or she will visit you in the dream to give you a drink of water.

CHAPTER 6

Animals Without Backbones

So far, all of the animals that have been mentioned are vertebrates. But there are enormous numbers of animals without backbones (invertebrates). This chapter cannot possibly include all of them. And besides, there are countless animals that are too small to be seen without a microscope. Before the microscope was invented, no one even knew they existed!

INSECTS

Insects have a hard outer covering, six legs, a three-part body, two antennae, and often two pairs of wings. The largest known insect is the

Goliath beetle, found in West Africa. It can be almost six inches long and can weigh more than three ounces. The smallest insect we know is probably a type of fairy fly that is only eight one-thousandths of an inch in length. It has a wingspan of four one-hundredths of an inch.

ANT

In ancient Mesopotamia, soldiers on guard were often told to watch the ants. If these insects were seen fighting, it meant that the enemy was approaching. And in the Ozarks there is a superstition that a baby who is slow to walk can be speeded up by smearing his or her legs with powdered black ants mixed with lard.

BEE

Bees are popular in the Ozarks. There is a saying there that you can always trust a beekeeper. If a honeybee buzzes around your head, you will receive a letter with money in it. In Malaya, on the other hand, if bees settle near your house it means bad luck.

These insects were also connected with

witchcraft. It was thought that if a captured witch ate a bee she would never confess her evil deeds.

In many parts of the world, it is thought that a piece of black cloth must be tied to a beehive when someone dies. If this is not done, the bees will stop making honey. In parts of France where people share this belief, it is also thought that a red cloth must be tied to the hive when there is happiness in the home.

In case you want to get rid of some bees, and don't live in Ireland, this is supposed to be a sure-fire trick. All you do is scatter a clod of soil from the Emerald Isle where they live.

BEETLE

Everyone knows the little verse about the ladybug, or ladybird. There are a few different versions, but one goes like this:

Ladybird, Ladybird, fly away home.
Your house is on fire and your children have gone.

Supposedly, if you quote this to a sitting ladybird, it will fly off in the direction of the

home of your true love. In parts of England and the United States, you should count the spots on this beetle. That will be the number of good months you will have in the coming year.

Some superstitions have to do with beetles in general. For example, any kind of beetle will cure whooping cough in the East Anglia part of England. Just tie the beetle to a thread and suspend it around the sick child's neck.

An Arab whose slave ran away could take a beetle of the same sex as the slave and tie it by a thread to a nail stuck in the ground. As the beetle crawls around the nail, the thread becomes shorter and shorter and the insect gets closer and closer to the nail. This is supposed to draw the slave back to the master.

The large stag beetle was thought to look like the Devil. That is why it was killed wherever it was seen in Scotland. Another evil beetle was the death-watch beetle. Its clicking was supposed to mean a death in the house.

BUTTERFLY

You might expect most of the superstitions about butterflies to be pleasant. After all, they are such beautiful insects. But such is not the case.

There is, of course, a belief in parts of England that seeing three butterflies flying together is lucky. And in Ireland, a butterfly flying around a corpse means that the dead person's soul has been saved.

But many more superstitions about butterflies are not that nice. In Bulgaria, just seeing a butterfly may mean that you will become sick. In parts of northern Europe, a butterfly flying at night means death.

Some Romanians used to teach their children that ghosts came back as butterflies. So it was all right to kill the insects. Perhaps the worst of all was the Swiss idea that butterflies can crawl into a man's brain through his ears and drive him crazy.

CATERPILLAR

In England, it was once the custom to carry a caterpillar around with you to keep from getting a fever.

CRICKET

In parts of Europe, if the crickets leave your house it means bad luck. But a cricket on the hearth means good luck.

DRAGONFLY

Sometimes the dragonfly is called a darning needle, or the Devil's darning needle. And it is thought that they can sew up the mouths of nagging wives or cursing husbands. On the South China coast, seeing a dragonfly may mean that a typhoon is approaching.

FIREFLY

In India it was thought that the firefly was carried by a bat back to its home. It was supposed to provide light for the bat children, since it was the only kind of light that they could stand. Some Japanese thought that an

The most magical caterpillar of all—the talking one in Alice in Wonderland.

ointment made of fireflies would prevent poisoning.

Possibly the strangest belief about fireflies comes from the Ozark mountains. If you can spit on a lightning bug as it is flying, you will have good eyesight all your life.

FLEA

There are places where it is thought that you can get rid of fleas by sticking pins in a piece of flannel clothing that you have been wearing, then burn the cloth. Or you can start a bonfire on Midsummer's Eve (the evening before the first day of summer) and jump over it.

LOUSE

In the Ozarks, if you find a louse on a baby's head, pick it up and put it in the family Bible. Slam the book shut, killing the louse, and make a wish about what profession you want the baby to follow. The wish will come true. But you can only do this once—no fair changing your mind!

MOTH

Another Ozark belief is that if a gray moth hovers over you, you will make money.

ARACHNIDS

This group, including spiders, mites, ticks, and scorpions, also has a hard outer covering. They have only two parts to their bodies and eight legs. The largest known spider is the bird-eating spider of South America. Its body can be three and one-half inches long and it can have a ten-inch leg span. The smallest known spider was found in Australia; it was one-thirty-fifth of an inch long.

SCORPION

The ancient Greeks thought that if you were bitten by a scorpion, you could use the animal itself as a cure. Pliny, a Greek writer, said, "It is thought good . . . to lay to the sore the same scorpion that did the harm; or to eat him roasted, and last of all to drink in two cups of pure wine of the grape."

SPIDER

In parts of Italy, the bite or sting of a tarantula was thought to cause *tarantism,* which is a hysterical disease in which the patient wants only to dance. A dance called the Tarantella was developed to serve as a cure for the disease.

Spiders can bring luck. In parts of England, if a golden spider crawls over your body, you will become rich. And there are Englishmen who hold a golden spider over their heads to make sure that they win in the football pools. Also in England, there is a saying, "If you would live and thrive, let a spider run alive." In the Ozarks, to have a red spider crawl on your clothing means you will make money.

Killing spiders can bring bad luck. In parts of England, killing a spider will cause a thunderstorm. And in Scotland and the West Indies, if you kill one you will break your dishes before the day is over.

Spiders have their medicinal purposes, too. To cure whooping cough, wrap a spider in raisins or butter or put it in a walnut shell. The

disease that they seem to be most connected with, however, is the ague. Victims of ague get a terrible fever that makes them sweat and get the chills in turn. You can cure this ailment by hanging three spiders around your neck, or one will do the trick if you have baked it first.

A nineteenth-century writer named Burton told this story:

> Being in the country in the vacation time, not many years since, at Lindly in Leicestershire, my father's house, I first observed this amulet of a *spider* in a nut-shell, wrapped in silk, so applied for an ague by my mother. . . . This I thought most absurd and ridiculous, and I could see no warrant in it . . . till at length, rambling amongst authors, I found this very medicine in Dioscorides, approved by Matthiolus, repeated by Aldrovandus. . . . I began to have a better opinion of it, and to give more credit to amulets, when I saw it in some parties answer to experience.

Even the webs of spiders have been used to cure the ague. And spiderwebs can, it is said, cure warts. But beware, according to an old Hebrew superstition, if a spiderweb falls down without a cause. That means a flood.

ONE LAST ANIMAL

The snail is a *mollusk* and so is a relative of the squid and the octopus. It can help a person find his or her true love, according to legend. On Hallowe'en, put a snail in a box. When you get up in the morning, look in the box. Supposedly, the snail will have traced with its slime the initials of your future husband or wife.

In the Ozarks, it is possible to make a wish on a snail. When you see one in the road, spit on his track and make a wish. But this only works if no one sees you do it.

Finally, these animals can be of medical aid, too. Rub a wart with a snail, then impale the snail on a thorn. As it dies, the wart will disappear. Even the slime of the snail was thought to cure consumption.

So there we have it. All over the world, from the dawn of time, people have believed strange things about the animals that they feared, that they loved, that they hated, and that they

respected. Even today, we all know of people who worry about black cats and common snakes, who carry a rabbit's foot, or who won't touch a toad. Perhaps everyone is a little bit superstitious.

Other Books About Animal Superstitions

Anonymous. *Encyclopedia of Magic and Superstition*. New York: Octopus Books, no date.

Baskin, Wade. *Dictionary of Satanism*. New York: Philosophical Library, Inc., 1972.

De Givry, Emile Grillot. *Picture Museum of Sorcery, Magic, and Alchemy*. New York: University Books, 1963.

Hill, Douglas, and Pat Williams. *The Supernatural*. New York: Hawthorn Books, Inc., 1965.

Hill, Douglas, et al. *Witchcraft, Magic and the Supernatural*. London: Octopus Books, 1974.

Randolph, Vance. *Ozark Magic and Folklore*. New York: Dover Publications, Inc., 1947.

Spence, Lewis. *An Encyclopaedia of Occultism*. New Hyde Park, N.Y.: University Books, 1960.

Trachtenberg, Joshua. *Jewish Magic and Superstition*. New York: Behrman's Jewish Book House, 1939.

Wedeck, Harry E. *Treasury of Witchcraft*. New York: Philosophical Library, Inc., 1961.

Index

Index

ABOUT THE AUTHOR

In more than thirty books, Thomas G. Aylesworth, Ph.D., has probed superstitions, the occult, and the mysteries of science. Among his books for McGraw-Hill are *The Story of Dragons and Other Monsters, The Story of Witches,* and *Who's Out There? The Search for Extraterrestrial Life.* Dr. Aylesworth has been a teacher, at Michigan State University and in public schools, and an editor, of *Current Science* magazine and children's books.

The author and his wife live in Stamford, Connecticut.

Animal Superstitions

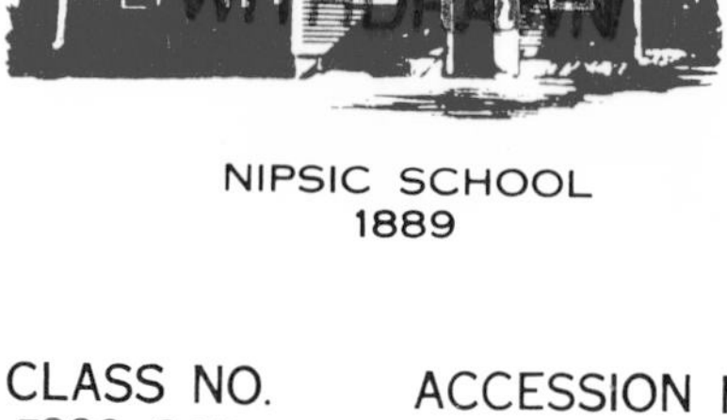

OTHER BOOKS BY THE AUTHOR

The Alchemists: Magic Into Science
Astrology and Foretelling the Future
Cars, Boats, Trains, and Planes of Today and Tomorrow
ESP
Geological Disasters: Earthquakes and Volcanoes
Graphology
Into the Mammal's World
It Works Like This
Monsters from the Movies
Movie Monsters
Mysteries from the Past
Palmistry
Science at the Ball Game
Science Update 77
Science Update 78
The Search for Life
Servants of the Devil
Storm Warning
The Story of Dragons and Other Monsters
The Story of Vampires
The Story of Werewolves
The Story of Witches
Teaching for Thinking
This Vital Air, This Vital Water
Traveling Into Tomorrow
Understanding Body Talk
Vampires and Other Ghosts
Werewolves and Other Monsters
Who's Out There?
The World of Microbes

Library of Congress Cataloging in Publication Data
Aylesworth, Thomas G Animal superstitions.
Bibliography: p. Includes index.
SUMMARY: Details superstitions about animals held in a variety of cultures in different epochs. 1. Animal lore—Juvenile literature. 2. Superstition—Juvenile literature. [1. Animal lore. 2. Superstition] I. Title.
GR820.A94 398'.369 80-21389
ISBN 0-07-0026658-0

1 2 3 4 5 6 7 8 9 BPBP 8 7 6 5 4 3 2 1

Animal Superstitions

THOMAS G. AYLESWORTH

Illustrated with photographs and old prints

McGRAW-HILL BOOK COMPANY
New York · St. Louis · San Francisco · Montreal · Toronto

Aylesworth, Thomas
Animal superstitions

Megan
Evans